Old Coldstream and Cornhill
by John Griffiths

This view of the bridge shows, on the left, the Marriage House, with little indication that the single storey front conceals a three storey building behind. The right hand building was restored in 1957. After 1753, when an Act of Parliament required parental consent for the marriage of persons younger than 21 years in England, until 1856, when Scots law was changed to require 21 days' residence by at least one of the prospective spouses, Coldstream, along with Lamberton Toll, Paxton Toll, Mordington Toll and Gretna Green, was a notorious spot for 'runaway marriages' - couples from England could be married instantly by unordained celebrants, including 'Patie Mudie', the dandified tailor Mr. McEwan, and the shoemaker Will Dixon who would customarily commence proceedings with the question "What's yer name my mon, an where d'ye come frae?". Despite three future Lord Chancellors of England marrying at Coldstream, the runaways were seldom elegant ladies and their gallants. Hastings M Neville, the long-serving Victorian and Edwardian Rector of Ford, asserted that Coldstream was a resort for drunken farm workers, who would often regret their bargain when sober; it seems more likely that the runaway weddings represent the continuation of a tradition of informal marriage in the English border counties. Instant weddings remained legal for Scottish residents until 1940.

© John Griffiths, 2007
First published in the United Kingdom, 2007,
by Stenlake Publishing Ltd.
www.stenlake.co.uk
ISBN 9781840334050

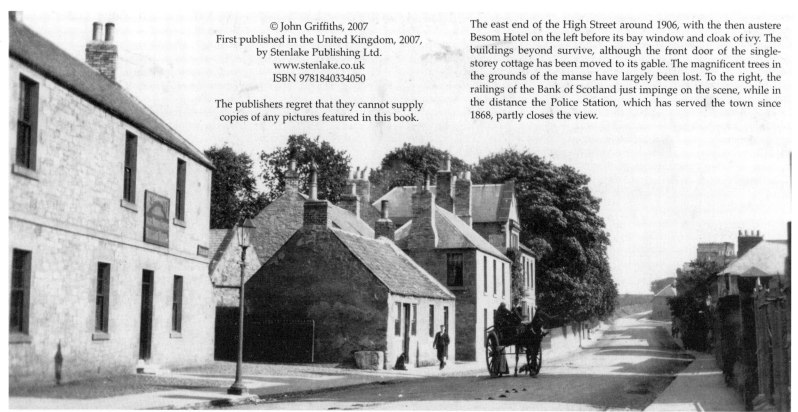

The east end of the High Street around 1906, with the then austere Besom Hotel on the left before its bay window and cloak of ivy. The buildings beyond survive, although the front door of the single-storey cottage has been moved to its gable. The magnificent trees in the grounds of the manse have largely been lost. To the right, the railings of the Bank of Scotland just impinge on the scene, while in the distance the Police Station, which has served the town since 1868, partly closes the view.

Further Reading

Kitty Cruft, John Dunbar & Richard Fawcett, *The Buildings of Scotland: Borders* (London 2006)

John Dent & Rory McDonald, *Farm and Factory: Revolution in the Borders* (Melrose 2001)

Dictionary of Scottish Architects: www.scottisharchitects.org.uk

Thomas Faulkner & Phoebe Lowery, *Lost Houses of Newcastle and Northumberland* (York 1996)

John Herdman (ed), *The Third Statistical Account of Scotland vol XXIII: The County of Berwick* (Edinburgh 1992)

Kelly's Directory of Northumberland 1906

Theo Lang, *The Border Counties* (London 1957)

Elizabeth Layke, *The History of Berwickshire's Towns and Villages* (Paxton 1994)

W.L.A. McCreath & B. Arthur, *A History of the Tweed Bridges Trust* (Berwick upon Tweed n.d.)

John James Mackay, *Border Highways* (Kelso 1998)

Maureen M. Meikle, *A British Frontier? Lairds and Gentlemen in the Eastern Borders, 1540-1603* (East Linton 2004)

Alistair Moffat, *The Borders* (Selkirk 2002)

Nikolaus Pevsner et al, *The Buildings of England: Northumberland* (2nd ed London 1992)

Rutherfurd's Southern Counties Register and Directory (1866; republished Selkirk 1990)

INTRODUCTION

As a trade route and economic resource, the river Tweed united rather than divided the districts on its banks, and was part of the sixth century Anglian kingdom of Bernicia, then part of the kingdom of Northumbria, which stretched from the Forth and the Solway to the Humber and the Mersey. It was attacked by the Norsemen, and as Wessex came to dominate the emerging English nation, was reduced to an Earldom. It was also squeezed from the north by the nascent Kingdom of Scotland. Lothian fell under Scottish sway, and following the Battle of Carham, on the banks of the Tweed near Wark, in 1023, the Borders region came to Scotland. In cultural terms, however, the people remained 'Borderers' as much as Scottish or English.

The region was a wild no-man's-land, without rule of law – where might was right, and reivers and moss-troopers ruled. Yet, it was not an undifferentiated whole. The east was markedly different from the central, where the Cheviot Hills served as a barrier between England and Scotland, or the west, where the estuarine flats and wetlands of the Solway served a similar function. The east was more settled, more agrarian, and, one might say, more urbane than the west. Carlisle was a fortress city, whilst Berwick, although heavily fortified, was a trading centre, and, until laid low by Edward I, was Scotland's richest port. Although the area covered in this book had its castles and fortified buildings, some incorporated into later dwellings, it also had sophisticated cross-border social networks. That these survived three centuries of conflict - open warfare or the rumbling sub-conflict of irregulars and bandits - testifies to the social and cultural links - a 'border identity'. The conflict culminated in 1513 with the Scottish king James IV's futile excursion into Northumberland in support of the French, then at war with the English king Henry VIII. Having reduced the border fortresses at Norham, Ford and Etal, James was overtaken by the Earl of Surrey and his army at Branxton - the Battle of Flodden. It was one of the bloodiest battles on British soil. As well as many thousands of footsoldiers, King James, and a large proportion of Scotland's ruling elite fell at Flodden, "Where shivered was fair Scotland's spear, And broken was her shield." The site is commemorated by a granite monument "To the Brave of Both Nations" and a recently laid out battlefield trail.

Neither the Union of the Crowns in 1603, nor the Act of Union of 1707, reduced the influence of prominent local families, it merely transformed their role from military to civil importance. North of the Tweed, the Earls of Home dominated, whilst to the south, the Earls, later Dukes, of Northumberland held sway. Numerous lesser gentry were also prominent, such as the Dicksons, Swintons and the Kers in Berwickshire, while in Northumberland Collingwoods, Herons, Forsters, Selbys and others led the transformation from war to peace.

Peace brought progress – whilst the Merse evolved into one of Scotland's most prosperous agricultural regions, Northumberland became renowned for its agricultural 'improvers'. William Roy's survey of Scotland in the 1740s-50s shows Berwickshire still organised for the old common field 'ridge and furrow' cultivation,

but increasingly the land on both sides of the border was enclosed into regular-shaped fields, and outlying farms, or 'ferm-touns' - farms with associated labourers' housing. Shelter belts of trees and commercial timber were planted in a hitherto tree-less region, while landowners invested in marling and liming their lands, field drainage, and experimentation with new crops and imported livestock. Along with improvements to land came developments in communications. The opening of Coldstream Bridge in 1766 improved the Newcastle-Edinburgh road - an Act of Parliament of 1762 provided for the turnpiking of Berwickshire's roads. Had the 1820 plan by the engineer Thomas Telford to build a road between the bridge and Greenlaw been implemented, Coldstream would have been by-passed, and very different today.

The Georgian period saw the building, and rebuilding, of country houses, in the classical style - including The Lees in 1770, and Lennel House in 1820. South of the border the frivolous Strawberry Hill Gothick was all the rage, exemplified by Ford Castle (1761-64, later rebuilt by Lady Waterford) and the great folly that was Twizel Castle (1770-1818), unfinished and now ruinous

Bereft of natural resources, other than soil and climate, industries were small-scale and ephemeral, although twentieth century Coldstream was noted for the manufacture of agricultural machinery. Likewise, the railway age made little impact. The Berwick-Kelso line of the North Eastern Railway passed through north Northumberland, although so far from Coldstream as to have little impact, and the rich agricultural land of the Merse was untouched by rail. From the 1870s the long agricultural depression struck cereal farming particularly hard; combined with increasing farm mechanisation, and the absence of other sources of employment, population figures fell. The region's population peaked in 1891 at 128,000 (in 2001 it was 107,000) - but included the textile towns and upland districts to the west. Many of the villages shown here saw much sharper falls in population, and the loss of village services such as shops and schools. Today, many of the villages are fortunate to retain a shop or pub, necessitating trips to Coldstream or Berwick. That was not yet the case when the bulk of the images in this book were made, from the late Victorian period to the 1920s. Here we see crowded school photographs, village streets with shops and inns and curious bystanders, as well as the bustling streets of Coldstream. But in some later pictures motor cars begin to appear, harbingers of a different kind of society. Particularly in the form of the motor bus they made travel much easier for ordinary people across the area: for work, for shopping, and, not least, for pleasure. It has been suggested that the provision of bus services allowing young people from local villages to experience the pleasures of the cinema or the dance hall in Berwick accounted for a twentieth century boom in cross-border marriages!

3

A large and interested crowd looks on as Provost Carmichael, accompanied by Bailie Proud, greets Mr Francis E. Wood (the bare-headed, white-bearded man at the centre of the crowd) outside Coldstream Town Hall on Friday 30 April 1926. Mr Wood, an 83-year-old Coldstream Guards veteran who had served between 1863 and 1870, was hoping to encourage regimental recruitment by walking from Wellington Barracks in London to Coldstream *and back*, having set off on 16 March with his 80 lbs of luggage in a hand-cart. This was not his first pedestrian adventure: the previous year he had flown to Paris (claiming to be the oldest man to have flown the Channel), and walked, via the Great War battlefields, to Brussels before flying home. His arrival in Coldstream was quite an event. Two Guards members – Lieutenant Russell and Sergeant Proud - were part of the welcoming party (one, in full dress uniform, can be seen in the Town Hall doorway), and Mr Wood was guest of honour at a smoking concert later that evening, where the Earl of Home, who was in the chair, described him as "a splendid example of British pluck". After spending the weekend at the Newcastle Arms Hotel as the guest of the local British Legion, and taking tea at The Hirsel on Sunday, he set off southwards again on Monday. The Town Hall shown here now houses the library and registrar's offices

The eastern end of Coldstream High Street around 1906, looking eastwards. From the left is the Town Hall; the protruding bay window of the Besom Hotel and, at the end (with the high gable), Dalgleish's motor dealership. The buildings on the right are Robert Scott, bookseller and stationer, George W. Gibson, photographer and postcard publisher (racks of cards are visible in his windows), R. Bruce, and the British Linen Company Bank, built in 1891. The space beyond the bank is occupied by a car park leading into Henderson Park, opened 1961, named in honour of the family of Coldstream doctors and laid out on the site of their tennis court . It contains an 18th century belvedere, and a monument to, and donated by, the Coldstream Guards, erected in 1968 when the Guards received the Freedom of the Burgh.

6th May 1935 was the Silver Jubilee of the accession to the throne of King George V, and as part of the celebrations in Coldstream a fancy dress parade was held. Here we can see some of the younger participants, headed by a pearly king and queen, waiting for the start beside the Bank of Scotland on Victoria Street. To the right of the photograph, the former Post Office can be seen, flying the Union Flag.

Coldstream's celebrations for the Coronation of King George VI, on Wednesday 12 May 1937, opened with a formal parade comprising police, the Boys' Brigade pipe band, Provost Angus with the magistrates and councillors, Territorials, ex-servicemen, Boys' Brigade, Girl Guides and Brownies, from the Town Hall to the Parish Church, where a service was held. Afterwards, the parade moved on to Home Park where Mrs George Walker, widow of a previous provost of Coldstream, planted a tree and was presented with a silver trowel by Lord Dunglass - the future Prime Minister Sir Alec Douglas-Home (1903-1995, PM 1963-64). In the afternoon, a fancy dress parade, starting at the Town Hall, proceeded via High Street, Market Place and Duns Road to Home Park. It is shown here mustering at Victoria Place, next to the Town Hall. Behind the Town Hall stands the Free Church, built in 1841 and extended in 1891, the additions including its landmark tower, donated by Thomas Hogg of Hope Park. It is now a bar. Behind the church stands the 1896-built house *Iolair*, with the new houses at the north end of Victoria Street completing the view.

Wednesday May 12, 1937 had been scheduled for the Coronation of King Edward VIII; following his abdication it was to serve for the Coronation of his brother, George VI. In Coldstream, the main celebrations took place at Home Park. Here, the fancy dress parade and competition is being judged. An eclectic range of entries, among the usual array of pierrots, Dutch girls and cowboys, included Jean Thompson (portraying 'Salad'), Pat Feurar ('Skipper Sardines'), Isobel Law ('Granny on her scooter'), Lockhart Elder ('O.H.M.S.') and the frankly inexplicable John Ford ('Henry has arrived'), who all won prizes. Unfortunately, grumbled the *Berwickshire News*, the parade was "not up to the high standard of the previous one, held on Jubilee Day, 1935" due to an outbreak of measles.

The fancy dress parade included three floats. This one, by the Coldstream branch of the S.W.R.I. and carried by local haulier Weathersons', was entitled 'The Visit of Margaret Tudor to Coldstream Abbey' and was, according to the *Berwickshire News*, "most effective and tasteful. Seated in her flower-bedecked alcove, 'Margaret Tudor', accompanied by her maid, and surrounded by nuns in their robes made an event in local history look most realistic." The other floats were by the 1st Coldstream Girl Guides, showing the works and training of the Guides, and the 'Coronation Bar', a mobile public house provided by the Coldstream Brewery Co. "The 'barman and his customers' provided the spectators with humour during the time the judging took place" recorded the paper. The low number of floats was explained by the Coronation having taken place on a Wednesday, in the middle of the working week.

The tower of Coldstream Parish Church dominates this 1920s view of central High Street. The church was constructed in 1716, replacing the one at Lennel, but was demolished, leaving the tower, in 1904 and rebuilt by 1908. The shop on the left is George Gibson & Son, printer and photographic supplier, and publisher of local postcards. Opposite, the railings at the extreme right are of the Bank of Scotland, now the residential home, Victoria Lodge. Beyond Nursery Lane, the curved frontage is now that of Coldstream Post Office, and the gabled building is now (2007) the butcher's shop of G.J.Sanderson. This westward view is closed by the Newcastle Arms Hotel.

R.Carmichael & Sons was a long established business when this 1920s view, looking westward along High Street, was taken: It was founded in 1832. The shop continues to trade as a grocer, but in its time it has been a seedsman and whisky blender - their brand being 'The Coldstream Guard'. Further along, is the nineteenth century Newcastle Arms Hotel, with the tower of the Perpendicular style West Church dominating the north side of the street. It was built in 1906-07 by the architect George Reavell of Alnwick for the United Presbyterian Congregation, changing its name to St Cuthbert's in 1950. It was secularised in 1963, and now houses the Coldstream Community Centre.

This view eastwards along the High Street is deceptive, as it hides the area's dominant building, the Parish Church. Halfway along the right hand side is R.Carmichael & Sons, and beyond it can be seen - just - the obelisk erected in front of the church in 1852 and dedicated to Sir John Marjoribanks of Lees, in gratitude "for his munificent gift of an abundant and permanent supply of water to the town" Beyond the obelisk is Young's hardware shop; two buildings down, and not visible, is the narrow alley named Gas Lane, leading to the former town gasworks. The nearest shop on the right, with the sign of a fish above the door, was William Crombie & Co's fish shop in the 1890s and is now (2007) Trotters the bakers; beyond, the property occupied by The Barber's Shop has lost its elaborate frontage.

Today, Coldstream's Market Place, down hill from the High Street, is a quiet residential backwater with few shops, but does boast the former headquarters of General George Monck's Regiment of Foot - the Coldstream Guards. Founded at Berwick in 1650, the Regiment fought for the Commonwealth at the Battle of Dunbar on 3 September that year. In late 1659 Monck - by now commander-in-chief of the army in Scotland - moved his headquarters to Coldstream, from where, on 1 January 1660, he marched on London, an action that led ultimately to the restoration of the monarchy. Monck (1608-1670) was honoured by Charles II, becoming Duke of Albermarle; his regiment, renamed the Coldstream Guards in 1670, maintains an institutional link between Cromwell's New Model Army and the British Army of today. The Headquarters Building in the illustration was restored in 1865, and in 1971 the Museum of Coldstream opened there. Its displays chronicle the history both of the regiment and the town.

A colour party of the 2nd Battalion, Coldstream Guards, parades in the Market Place in front of Provost Carmichael and other dignitaries, on Tuesday, 6 September 1921. The occasion was the prsenting of the former colours of the battalion to the Burgh of Coldstream, to be kept in the parish church (King George V had recently presented new colours to the 3 battalions of the regiment). The picture shows the Regimental Colours to the left and the King's Colours to the right; Provost Carmichael is standing just right of the King's Colours; the figure to the left in scarlet and ermine robes, despite his glorious raiment, is merely a guest: Provost Fair, of Duns. The senior officer present was Lt. Gen Sir Alfred Codrington, colonel of the regiment, who may be the figure addressing Provost Carmichael, and the colour party was commanded by Colonel H. Studd. After the ceremonies in the Market Place, the troops and officials marched in procession to the Parish Church, following which there were more informal ceremonies: lunch in the Mechanics' Hall, and a cricket match in which the guards were trounced by the town, the latter including Lord Dunglass (Sir Alec Douglas-Home).

The River Tweed photographed from the Nuns Walk - which commemorates the Cistercian Nunnery established at Coldstream by Earl Gospatrick in 1165, burned by the Earl of Hertford in 1545, and finally demolished in 1621. To the left of Coldstream Bridge is the 70 feet column topped by a statue of Charles Albany of Marjoribanks of The Lees, Liberal Member of Parliament for Berwickshire between 1832 and 1834). It was erected by local Liberals in 1834 to celebrate the passing of the Reform Act in 1832 and Marjoribanks' 'high talents, amiable qualities and political principles'. 'Charlie' - the stone version - was struck down by lightning in 1873, but replaced the following year.

These semi-detached houses on Home Terrace, part of Duns Road, were among the 78 houses built by Coldstream Burgh Council between the wars. The 1919 Housing Act and its successors obliged local authorities to provide housing. The ones pictured here are typical of the 'low density' housing of that era - twelve houses to the acre according to the influential theories of the planner and architect Raymond Unwin, with sizeable front and rear gardens. Many are now privately owned. The name Home Terrace derives from the Earls of Home whose seat, The Hirsel, lies a mile west of the town. The earldom was created in 1605, and its best-known incumbent was the 14th Earl, who, renouncing his peerage, was Sir Alec Douglas-Home, Prime Minister in 1963-64.

Coldstream Cottage Hospital, opened on 29 December 1888 and shown here around 1906, with the postman and his sack of letters. The gazebos in the hospital gardens provided fresh air, and shelter, for patients. The hospital was designed by John McLachlan of Edinburgh (who had designed the hospitals at Hawick and Selkirk) and cost £1,841.0s.11d, raised by a bazaar, sales of work, and donations, not least from Maria, Countess of Home (d.1919) who was a leading sponsor of the project. A dispensary was added later, and the hospital had a maternity ward between 1951 and 1988. It continues to serve the people of the district, sometimes in rather surprising ways: in its early days, when a local vagrant called Dick Turpin was seen in the neighbourhood, the matron would send out nurses to apprehend him, give him a bath and cut his toenails. Next to the hospital, a health centre opened in 1976. The front gardens are now taken up by a car park.

A fine turn-out of collectors for Heather Day, the annual flag day of the Scottish Children's League of Pity, the junior branch of the National Scottish Society for the Prevention of Cruelty to Children. The League of Pity was established in 1893, but the first Heather Day took place in 1912. 'Help Suffering Children' runs the slogan on the posters, and the efforts of the female collectors are bolstered by those of two cycle-borne Boy Scouts. The bicycling lady at the left of the photograph looks as if she wished she were elsewhere.

This image, from the late 1920s, shows boys bathing in the Leet Water, while other children, perched precariously on a nearby wall, look on. The Leet Water rises north of Swinton, passing Leitholm (the village is named after the river) and flows across the flat countryside of the Merse before entering the River Tweed at Coldstream. Here it is seen passing under the Leet Bridge, at the western end of Coldstream, which carries the Coldstream to Kelso road (now the A698). The Leet was known as a fine trout river, which also, records Rutherfurd's Directory, contained pike and "very large eels".

The buildings in this view of Lennel are virtually unchanged, although the two-storeyed house to the left has had a bay window added, and the cottage in the centre of the photograph - the Salmon Inn, run by David Renton - no longer functions as licensed premises. This settlement was originally known as Lennel Newtown. The original village of Lennel, destroyed during the Anglo-Scottish wars which raged during the medieval and early modern era, stood to the west around its ancient church, the ruins of which still stand in its churchyard. Until 1716 (when Coldstream parish church was built), Coldstream parish was known as Lennel or Leinhall.

The classical mansion Milne Graden House, overlooking the River Tweed south of Ladykirk, was built in 1822 for Admiral Sir David Milne (1763-1845), and subsequently the home of his eldest son, David Milne Home (1805-1890). He gave up a law practice, on succeeding to the estate, but later achieved prominence in the fields of geology and meteorology. On his death, it came to his daughter, Miss Jane Milne Home. The house was designed by the energetic and versatile James Gillespie Graham (1776-1855), who built mansions, banks and churches the length of Scotland and in a variety of styles - Jacobean, Gothic, and 'Gothick' as well as classical; and he is thought to have pioneered the term 'baronial' for the characteristic nineteenth century Scottish architectural form.

  Having lost many of its commercial outlets, Leitholm is now a quiet village on the Berwick to Kelso road (B6461). Included in the losses are the shops shown on this image from around 1930: Thompson's store, with the advertisement for Wills's 'Bulwark' tobacco in the front garden, and which also provided 'teas and refreshments', now a private house, and E.Brown's garage and petrol station, with cottage (demolished 2006). With pumps dispensing Shell, BP and Pratt's fuels, Mr Brown was catering for many tastes! The single-storey cottages at the left have also been demolished although the Plough Hotel (dating from around 1800, visible just beyond the petrol pumps) has survived. The village had two public houses, the now-defunct Black Horse, situated towards the west end of the village, and The Plough, at the time of this photograph, run by Robert White. Leitholm was situated in the parish of Eccles - of which it was the largest village, and, according to Rutherfurd's County Directory of 1866, "much pleasanter" than Eccles itself, with "the houses being superior, and having some very good shops". In its regular layout along both sides of the broad, straight main street, the village shows signs of having been planned or 'improved' in the course of its history.

This rather more sedate photograph was taken from some yards further west along Leitholm's main street, and a couple of decades earlier, in the mid Edwardian period. The single-storey cottages are those shown at the left-hand of the previous image (the rustic fence of criss-crossed poles is the same), while the building immediately beyond the projecting wooden shed on the right is Thompson's shop. Like many rural villages in the Merse, Leitholm lacked a mains water supply until the 1950s, being until then reliant on 22 wells.

Leitholm school could accommodate 119 pupils in the 1880s. It closed in 1980 and has been demolished, the modern houses of School Wynd have been built on its site. Leitholm's primary school age children now travel to the 1960s Eccles Leitholm Primary School in Eccles.

Leitholm

Belchester, a few hundred yards south east of Leitholm, has been home to the Dickson family since the 14th century. The house, of course, has been altered and extended many times over the centuries, having been built, originally, as a tower. In 1588 John Dickson of Belchester murdered his father before fleeing to England. He was brought back in 1591, tried and condemned at Edinburgh and executed by torture. According to a contemporary chronicler, Dickson was, *brought to the scaffold, and at the cross broken on ane rack ... where he lay all that night, and on the morn carried to the gallows of the Burgh-moor, where the rack was set up, and the corpse laid thereupon.*

The children of Eccles outside their school on the Birgham road around 1906. The school, built in the 1880s, to accommodate 114 children; has been demolished and a modern school serving Eccles and Leitholm built on the site. The large house in the trees beyond was the Free Church manse. Rutherfurd's Directory of 1866 describes Eccles, somewhat unfairly, as "consisting of one street, and resembling any other country village". The name Eccles, deriving from the Latin ecclesia via the British *egles*, 'church', indicates a very early origin, and was the site of a nunnery founded by Earl Gospatrick in 1155, but burned down by Hertford in 1545 during the 'Rough Wooing' campaign brought about by Henry VIII's desire to force the marriage of his heir Edward to Mary Queen of Scots, and thus unite the crowns of England and Scotland. Eccles parish church, dedicated originally to St Cuthbert and later to St Andrew, was rebuilt in 1774 and stands behind the wall on the left.

Right: Eccles House, home to the Greig family, was built in a 'Scottish Renaissance' style by architects Leadbetter & Fairley in 1898, replacing an earlier building.

Below: A row of farm cottages in Eccles, photographed by W.H.Simpson of Kelso around 1906, eloquently displays the difference between 'model' cottages with gables, high ceilings, ample chimneys and slate roofs, and the lower, tile-roofed cottage closer to the viewer.

Cycling had become a popular recreation by the turn of the twentieth century, and the refreshment rooms shown in this mid-Edwardian image, run by I. Wood, seem to have been a popular halt. 'Go to Birgham' used to be a popular term of reproach, but whether in commemoration of some act of ignominy which took place here, or as a reference to the village's perceived isolation is unclear. Birgham is noted in history for the 1290 Treaty of Birgham, when it was agreed that Edward I's son, Edward , the Prince of Wales, should marry Margaret, the Maid of Norway, without any diminution of Scottish 'rights, liberties and customs'. Unfortunately, the Maid died while travelling to Scotland. The traveller Edward Bogg, writing in 1898, was not impressed by Birgham, believing it to have "a somewhat dingy, dirty, melancholy, and desolate aspect."

A splendid Gypsy caravan rumbles eastwards through Birgham towards Coldstream, watched by two lady cyclists and a number of men. The Borders had a significant Gypsy population, centred on the nearby village of Yetholm. The buildings shown here survive (with the exception of the pantiled cottage behind the caravan), as does the telegraph pole! The magnificent stable block forms an appropriate backdrop for this most interesting image.

Cornhill's main street now forms part of the A697 road between Newcastle, Coldstream and Edinburgh and is frequently busy with through traffic. A much more peaceful scene is shown here! The two large trees in the centre of the image now tower over the Collingwood Arms (left), named for the Lords of the Manor, the Collingwood family of Cornhill House; at the time this photograph, around 1906, the licensee was a Mrs Mary McLachlan. The village shop and adjoining cottages shown in the next image stand behind the trees. The chained area where the photographer stood is now occupied by Cornhill's War Memorial. The road through Cornhill and Coldstream had been a busy route during the coaching era, but whereas Coldstream never developed large coaching inns, the Collingwood Arms profited from the passing trade, and still boasts the words 'Posting Horses' on its porch. On the extreme right is the edge of the churchyard of St Helen's parish church.

Cornhill Village shop, around 1906, when it was run by Nicholas Jeffrey, still occupies the building at the left of this photograph, and the two adjacent cottages still stand, the second of them being the village's Police House, occupied in the Edwardian period by Constable William Crisp . The more distant cottages, including Cornhill's then Post Office, managed in 1906 by Miss Ann Reid, the sub-postmistress, have been replaced by modern bungalows.

The staff at Coldstream Railway Station pose for the camera in 1908, when the stationmaster was John Paterson. On the North Eastern Railway's Tweedmouth to Kelso line, Coldstream's station was unusual - not only was it not in the town for which it was named, but was not even in the same country, being well over a mile to the east, across the Tweed at Cornhill in England. The line was opened in 1849, and Cornhill, or Coldstream, gained further importance in 1887 when the NER opened the Coldstream branch line from Alnwick, running through Wooler to join the Kelso line just south of Coldstream station. Apart from two platforms, the station had a turntable, engine shed, and sidings serving the adjacent auction market, of which the sales ring can still be seen. Passenger services on the Tweed Valley line ended in June 1964, but a goods service from Tweedmouth to Kelso lasted until March 1965. The station site is now occupied by housing.

Cornhill

The roadside settlement Donaldson's Lodge stands in Cornhill parish between Cornhill and Berwick. This view looks north-eastwards along the main road, now the A698. Of the buildings shown here, only the two-storeyed house of the row, right of the road, 'Donaldson's Lodge', and the 1893 Primitive Methodist chapel, to the left, still stand. In the mid 19th century the hamlet also boasted a public house, the Plough Inn, beyond the chapel, but this, too, has gone. Apart from the chapel, the hamlet also had a shop, run in 1906 by Andrew Easton.

The sixteenth-century Twizel Bridge spans the River Till, overlooked by Twizel Castle. The castle was built, around the core of a medieval building, by Sir Francis Blake, Bt. (1737-1818) between 1770 and his death in 1818, in the then fashionable Gothick style at a cost of around £80,000. The local antiquary Canon Raine was not impressed, describing the castle, in 1852, as; *a melancholy memorial of the most extreme want of taste and the most needless profusion*. Sir Francis' heirs abandoned the place, preferring to live at nearby Tillmouth Park. Twizel Bridge was an engineering marvel of its day. Dating from the 1509-11, and designed by master mason Christopher Scune, it crosses the River Till with a spectacular 90 ft span arch, the largest single span stone arch bridge in Britain until that record was claimed by the Causey Arch, Co Durham, in 1727. The bridge was wide and strong enough to carry heavy artillery pieces, and played a significant role in the Flodden campaign of 1513, allowing Surrey's English army to cross the Till with ease as they marched north in a flanking movement to engage the Scottish army of James IV.

Twizel Bridge

An Edwardian photograph of Tillmouth Park, built by Francis Douglas Blake (1856-1940, created a Baronet in 1907) in 1882 on the site of an earlier 'Tillmouth Park' house, built in 1810 by Sir Francis Blake (1737-1818), who had also built Twizel Castle. This building was designed by Charles Barry jnr (son of Charles Barry, the architect of the Palace of Westminster), who employed the Elizabethan style - then deemed the most appropriate for country house design - and is typified by large windows, hood moulds above the apertures, and high chimneys. Stone from Twizel Castle is said to have been used in its construction. It is surrounded by gardens and grounds laid out by Sir Francis in 1810, including archways, a bridge and a tunnel and an incomplete bridge over the River Till. The Blake family sold the house and estate in 1955; the house is now a country house hotel.

Norham Bridge - officially Norham and Ladykirk Bridge - was built 1885-87 by the Tweed Bridges Trust (established 1884) and designed by the engineer Cuthbert Brereton (1850-1910) and Thomas Coddrington. Brereton worked on dock and railway projects in south Wales, was engineer for a number of London Underground lines, and designed Kew Bridge over the Thames. Norham Bridge replaced an earlier timber structure, opened in 1830; Brereton made use of the stone abutments created for this earlier bridge, replacing its two wood lattice arches with four masonry arches constructed by Messrs Meakin and Dean of Glanton, Northumberland. The view remains virtually unchanged, although the cabbage patch to the right is now a lay-by for anglers, and the pump by the toll-house has been removed. Norham Castle can just be seen on the horizon in the centre of the shot, and the tree at the right hand edge is still there.

Norham Bridge

Norham's medieval market cross dominates this 1905 view of the small Tweedside market town, with Castle Street behind and the castle itself visible above trees at the end of the street. The cross has medieval steps and column; the conical top was added in 1870, and the weathervane on top now takes the appropriate shape of a salmon.. Both the Victoria Hotel - left of the village cross, with signboard, and run in 1906 by James Shiel - and Foreman's Butchers (the first complete building shown on the right) run then by Henry Foreman - remain in business as they were in the Edwardian period.

English Heritage do not appreciate trees growing on their buildings and so it, and the rickety fence, have been cleared away, but otherwise this view of Norham Castle is unchanged. The castle was first built in 1121 by the fiery Ranulph Flambard, Bishop of Durham, and rebuilt by succeeding bishops, most notably by Hugh Puiset in the late 12th century. Episodes in its lively career include being twice captured by King David of Scotland in his efforts to annex north-east England, and again by James IV prior to Flodden. In 1559 the castle was acquired by the English crown from the Bishopric of Durham and was partly rebuilt as an artillery fort. Norham itself was a small borough by the second half of the 12th century; it superseded the adjacent and now deserted village of Ubbanford and was 'capital' of Norhamshire, a detached portion of County Durham, which, with Islandshire (Holy Island and adjacent districts) and Bedlingtonshire, was only incorporated formally into Northumberland in 1844.

Norham Castle

The tall buildings at the left of the row, including in 1860 the Swan Inn, have since been demolished, and the low row of cottages substantially rebuilt, although they can be identified by the positioning of their chimneys. Now a small hamlet, Duddo was large enough to gain a chapel of ease (dependent on Norham) in 1832 and became a separate parish in 1864. A new church was built in 1880, the former church building being thereafter used as a National School.

Duddo.

Above: The ruins of Duddo Tower can be seen here in all their glory; their impact today is somewhat diminished by the trees which now cover much of the crag on which the tower stands. The tower was a late construction, dating from the 16th or early 17th century, a previous tower having been destroyed in 1496 by James IV during a raid into northern England.

Below: These were recorded as 'Duddo Four Stones' on the 1860 Ordnance Survey map, and recorded as 'four monolithic stones' in Kelly's Directory of 1906, though five are clearly visible in the image, dated 1905. Canon Raine, a prominent local antiquarian, noted four stones standing in 1852, with a fifth extended upon the ground, in a broken state; it has since been raised. Excavation has indicated that there may have been a total of seven stones. The five standing stones, rubbed smooth around the bases by livestock, look like so many clenched fists. The tallest is around 2.2m high and the circle has a diameter of around 10m.

Duddo

Etal village, shown here around 1905, was noted for its large number of thatched cottages - a rare survival in Edwardian Northumberland. The largest building, and the structure immediately to its left, form the Black Bull; in 1906 the licensee was Leonard Stonehouse. It is still in business and Northumberland's only thatched public house. The other cottages were demolished and replaced by slate-roofed buildings in the 1920s and 30s by the Joicey family, coal-owners, which acquired the Etal and Ford estates in 1907; so sensitively were these designed, however, that the village has retained its considerable charm. In the distance is Etal Castle, dating from the late 13th or early 14th centuries, and given 'licence to crenellate' (to be fortified) in 1342. It was one of a trio of castles (with Norham and Ford) captured by James IV between his invasion of England in the last week of August 1513 and his defeat and death at Flodden on 9 September 1513.

This appears to be the village tailor of Ford, Samuel Smith (c.1840-1923), and his wife Margaret (*nee* Gray), who he married in 1872. Samuel had inherited the business from his father, also Samuel Smith; in the Edwardian period he worked alongside his younger brother William George Smith, who later took over the business. Hastings Neville, Rector of Ford, referred to the Smiths in his *A Corner in the North* (1909): *We still have the village tailor. There is now work for one or two tailors in a parish which used to keep six or seven busily engaged.* Village tailors in the nineteenth century would mainly carry out their trade at the homes of their customers, a practice known as "whipping the cat", but more or less defunct by the turn of the century.

Ford Castle was another of the border strongholds captured by James IV in his ill-fated Flodden campaign of 1513. The castle was built in the 14th century by Sir William Heron, but extensively rebuilt in succeeding centuries, most notably given a 'Gothick' style by Sir John Hussey Delaval (1728-1808) in the late eighteenth century. Hussey was a member of the landowning and industrialist family which had built the port of Seaton Delaval in Northumberland; Sir John also enclosed and improved his lands and tenant farms at Ford. The castle was subsequently given a 'Baronial' architectural makeover, as shown here, by the Marchioness of Waterford in the early 1860s. Louisa, Marchioness of Waterford (1818-1891) had made Ford Castle her main home following the death of her husband, the 3rd Marquess, in a riding accident in 1859, and devoted the rest of her life to 'religion, philanthropy and art'. The Waterford's had acquired Ford by inheritance from the Delavals in 1822. The estate was sold to the first Lord Joicey in 1907.

Blacksmith Shop, Ford

As well as remodelling Ford Castle, Lady Waterford devoted much of her considerable energy to rebuilding and improving Ford village. Picturesque model cottages were built, the village inn (built by Sir John Hussey Delaval) was closed, and a school was built and embellished with Biblical paintings by the Marchioness (no longer a school and now the Lady Waterford Gallery). Perhaps the best known building in the village is the smithy, with its distinctive horseshoe door, rebuilt in 1863. In 1897 it was occupied by Ralph Hutchinson for an annual rental of £7. An anvil can be seen by the doorway, together with a plough, perhaps awaiting repair. Ford's drinkers were subsequently catered for by a canny entrepreneur who opened a beer house just over the parish boundary, in Barmoor and outside the Marchioness' sway.

Crookham, recorded as Crucum in 1244, derives from Old Scandinavian 'at the bends' (of the nearby River Till), but it could equally apply to its winding village street. The buildings shown have been modified, but the single storey cottage protruding into the gap between the two larger houses is the village post office, and the curving wall on the left encloses the school, which also housed Anglican services. The village appears to be decked out for some day of celebration. The sheep being driven along the street give an indication of Crookham's agricultural provenance. In 1906 its inhabitants included Richard Curle at the Post Office, Walter Scott, tailor, and, perhaps unusually, a lady butcher, Mrs Mary Robson. Although Crookham formed part of the Ford estate, and Lady Waterford built cottages here, its inn, the Blue Bell (or Bluebell) was left alone, being run at this time by George Young, who was also a farmer.

Branxton is the closest village to the battlefield of Flodden. This view, taken around 1906, shows the west end of the village, the road dividing for Cornhill (right) and the Flodden Memorial (left). The white cottage at the end of the left hand row survives, with an added porch; as do the buildings in the centre of the photograph. However, the cottage on the right has been replaced by the village hall. The tower of Branxton Church, rebuilt in 1849, can just be made out behind the tree right of the central group of buildings.

Although this Edwardian-era photograph claims to be of the 'Actual Battlefield of Flodden' it was taken from the site of the battle memorial facing away from the scene of most of the action. Instead we have a panoramic view of Branxton village, with the church at the western end. Dedicated to St Paul, this was built in 1849, but incorporates much older material: Norman stonework and a 13th century chancel arch. In 1906 the incumbent was the Revd. Charles Ernest Hoyle, M.A. English and Scottish victims of the Battle of Flodden are buried in its churchyard.

Below: Drink, weary pilgrim, drink and stay / Rest by the well of Sybil Grey, runs the inscription on this elaborate well, high on Flodden Hill, in what is now Flodden Quarry Nature Reserve, and was commissioned by Louisa, Lady Waterford in the 1880s. The Well features in Sir Walter Scott's poem Marmion (1808). Scott's anti-hero Lord Marmion, after a series of journeys and adventures, takes part in the Battle of Flodden, is killed and is buried at the spot; the well is described in the poem as; *A little fountain cell, Where water, clear as diamond spark,/ In a stone basin fell. / Above, some half-worn letters say, Drink, weary pilgrim, drink and pray, / For the kind soul of Sybil Grey, / Who built this cross and well.* Doubtless Louisa thought she could improve on Scott. However, it is thought that the well on which Scott based his lines was elsewhere, and that this was originally 'the Soldiers' Well', named after the Scots troops encamped here before Flodden. Here their heavy artillery was dug in to counter an attack from the south, but the wide outflanking advance of the English under the Earl of Surrey led James IV to the fateful decision to move his army from Flodden Hill to Branxton Hill to the north, and there to do battle with the English.

Left: "To the Brave of Both Nations" is the conciliatory epitaph on the Flodden Memorial, erected by the Berwickshire Naturalists Club and unveiled on 27 September 1910 by the author and poet Sir George Douglas, Bart, on the centre of the English battle line of 9 September 1513. The Scots stood a little to the south, on the northern slope of Branxton Hill. A belt of marshy ground proved fatal to the advancing Scots pikemen who became bogged down and prey to billhook-wielding English troops. Casualties cannot easily be determined, but Flodden was one of the bloodiest battles ever fought on British soil. The Scots lost their king, James IV, his son who was the Archbishop of St Andrews, two abbots, 11 earls, 15 lords and many thousand other soldiers.